MANSA MUSA: THE RICHEST MAN IN HISTORY

Mike McCraw

STORY TIME LINES

Ruler, scholar, statesman, and devout man of faith; Mansa Musa was a **14th century African emperor** who reigned over the **Mali Empire** from **1312 to 1337**.

Musa was **born to Kankou and Faga Laye in 1280**. Though it has been said that Musa did, indeed, have some blood ties to the throne, his father was never emperor. This means he **did not inherit the throne by birth right** which is common in many kingdoms.

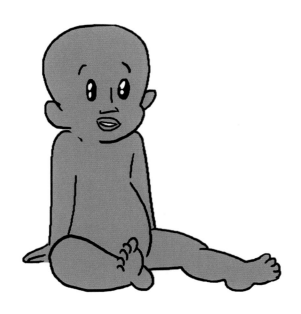

1280

Sometime **in 1310 Musa became the Kankoro-Sigui**, a type of deputy or apprentice **to Mansa Abubakari Keita II**.

1310

In the following year, Mansa Abubakari set sail to explore the limits of the Atlantic Ocean, **leaving Musa in charge**.

1311

Well...a whole year went by and Mansa Abubakari had not returned.

1312

Unable to locate Abubakari, **in 1312**, Musa ascended to the throne and **became Mansa Musa**. "Mansa" meaning **"emperor"** or **"king of kings"**.

1312

As emperor, Mansa Musa's negotiations with outside empires lead to the expansion of trade between states **north** of the Sahara Desert...

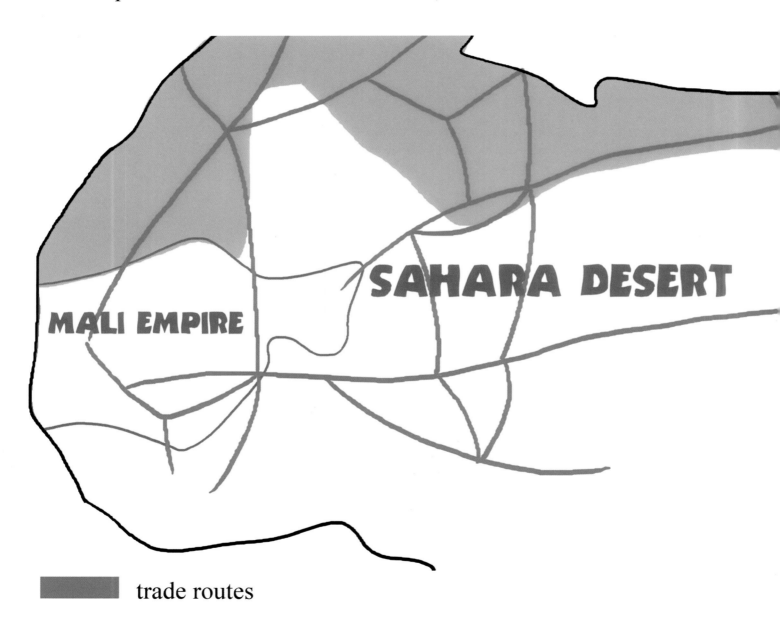

trade routes

...and states **south** of the Sahara Desert.

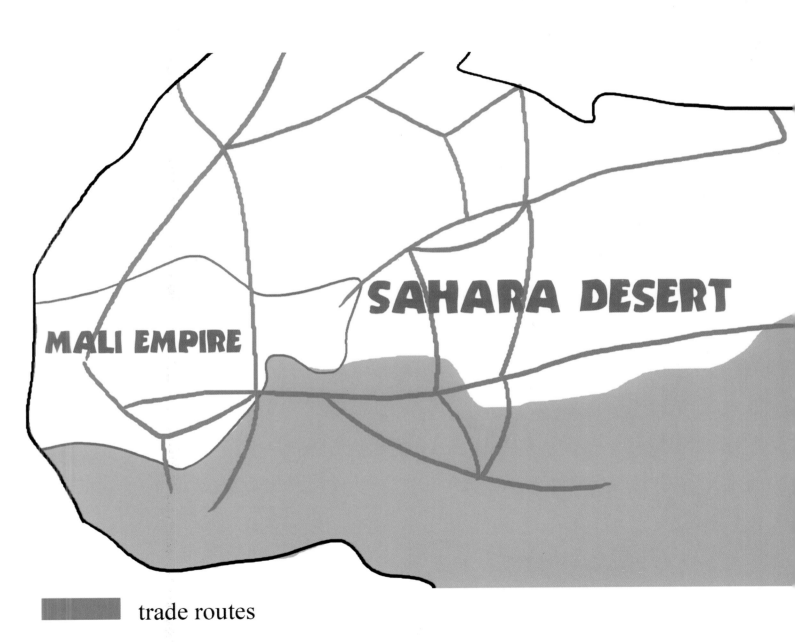

MALI EMPIRE

SAHARA DESERT

trade routes

Mali was in **control of these trade routes** due to their geographic positioning.

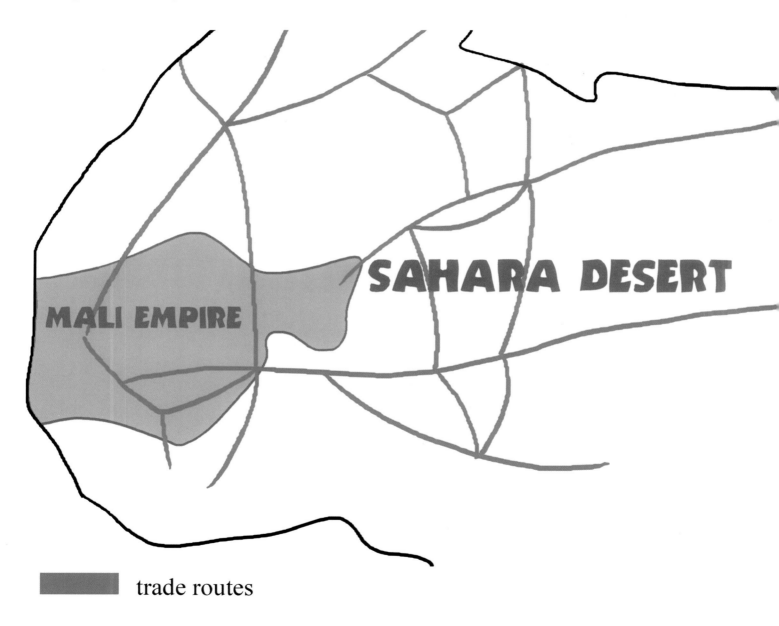

trade routes

That means Mali was moving everything from **textiles**...

...metal instruments...

...kola nuts...

...slaves...yes...slaves...

...not to mention the much coveted **salt** and...

...wait for it...

...**gold**. That's right. The mineral that was the **backbone of international commerce**. Mali was in control of the **largest supply** known at the time. Making Mali the richest empire in the world and making **Mansa Musa the richest man of all time**.

Aside from being a successful diplomat, Mansa Musa has been described as **strong, yet fair**. He's been credited with uniting Mali and all of it's regions under one fair legal system and one religion...

...Islam.

Though it's been stated that Mansa Musa limited access of markets along the Niger River to only Muslims, a point is repeatedly made in reports of his life that even though he governed under Islam, nobody was ever forced to abandon their beliefs by the state.

A faithful Muslim himself, Mansa Musa decided to take his **mandatory pilgrimage to Mecca**, known as **the Hajj**, in **1324**.

1324

Going back to how Musa became Emperor, we know that kings taking off for a period of time isn't unusual. Also, Muslim men have accepted that, if able, **they must take the Hajj at least once before they die**. So, there's nothing extraordinary about Mansa Musa taking off for the Hajj. But the **way** he took the Hajj was very extraordinary.

1324

Mansa Musa left Mali for Mecca with a caravan of **60,000 men covered in fine silk, holding golden staffs**...

1324

...80 to 100 camels, each one carrying **300 pounds of gold**.

1324

His wife even had an entourage of **500 people** of her own.

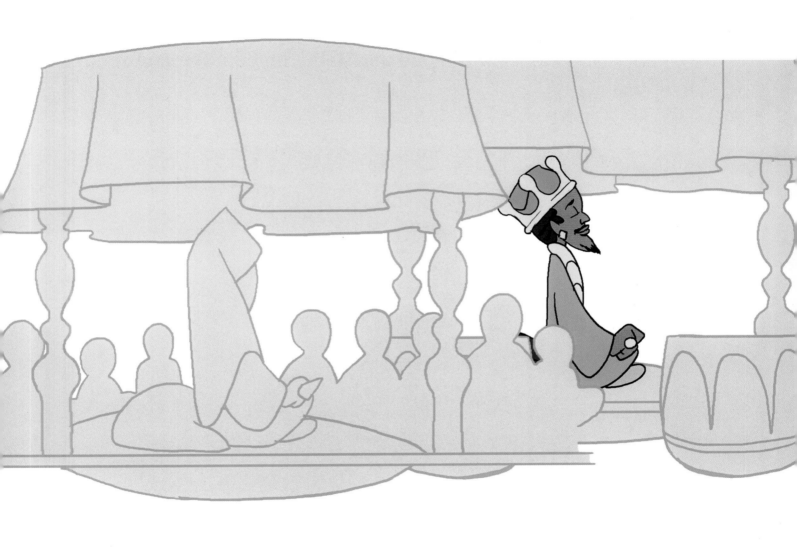

1324

Not just that, but as they passed through towns, Mansa Musa and his aids **handed out an unimaginable amount of gold** to...pretty much everyone. Poor and rich alike. Needless to say, this extravagant show of wealth made Mansa Musa and the Mali Kingdom **international celebrities**.

1324

Due to Mansa Musa's generosity, there was so much gold in **Cairo, Medina, and Mecca**, that the value of gold in these regions actually dropped. **Causing a depression** in Cairo, Medina, and Mecca that lasted for **over a decade**.

Yes, Mansa Musa gave out so much money that **he broke national economies**.

Aside from flooding the streets with gold, **Mansa Musa found some of the best scientists, architects, and scholars** and brought them back to Mali with him. His goal was to increase his kingdom's prosperity through **education and construction**.

Though **Niani** was Mali's capital, Mansa Musa spent the years after his return from the Hajj building up **Timbuktu** as an epicenter for **commerce and education**.

Timbuktu is where he constructed great centers of learning like the **Sankore Madrasah** which, at one point, had **one of the largest collections of books** in the world.

As well as the **Djinguereber Mosque** which still stands to this day.

Nobody seems quite sure as to when Mansa Musa died, but it is widely accepted that after **1337**, Mansa Musa was Mansa no more, being succeeded by his son.

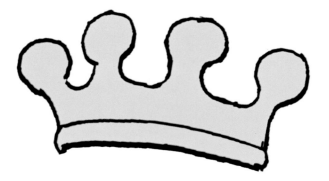

1337

After all of his accomplishments as the emperor of Mali, Mansa Musa's status as an international celebrity came back around when **foreign cartographers**, began depicting his image and noting his name on maps of Africa. Mansa Musa literally **put Mali and himself on the map**.

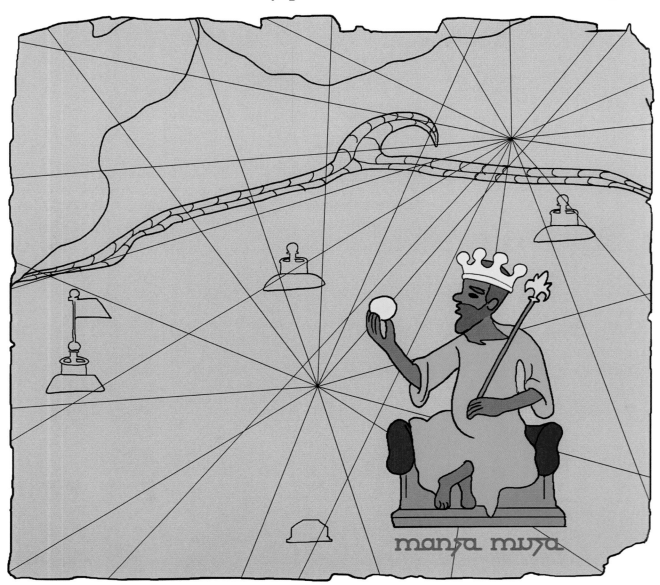

Diplomacy, wealth, knowledge and faith are all things seemingly important to and characteristic of the great Emperor of Mali, **Mansa Musa**. This is just a small peek into what is known and currently being discovered about the man, **Mansa Musa and his timeline**.

STORY TIME LINES

Made in the USA
Middletown, DE
11 August 2020